Miami Flor

2023-2024

How to Experience Miami's Stunning Glamor: Must-See Attractions, Perfect Beaches, and Hidden Side Attractions.

Rafael M. Stones

Table of Content

INTRODUCTION

Miami, a city that seduces visitors with its enticing combination of sun, surf, and vibrant culture, is proof of the attraction of the American tropics. This city, located in the heart of South Florida, constantly defies expectations. Miami is a city unlike any other, with its distinctive pastel-hued Art Deco buildings on South Beach and the rhythmic sway of salsa and merengue filling the air at night.

Your key to discovering the wonders of this vibrant city is this Miami Travel Guide. This will serve as your guide on a journey into the heart of Miami, whether you're visiting for the first time or coming back to explore more of its mysteries.

This travel guide is an invitation to really experience Miami, not just a list of statistics and information. We'll guide you through the must-see landmarks that shape the skyline, culture, and history of the city. Each chapter delves deeper into the colorful fabric of Miami life. We've got everything covered, from the famous beaches and cultural centers to the obscure side attractions that showcase the city's true personality.

This will assist you in making day-by-day plans as you begin your Miami adventure to make sure you don't miss the unique opportunities Miami offers. We'll give you a little history lesson on Little Havana, where authentic Cuban cuisine and customs are alive and well. As street art and galleries converge in Wynwood, you'll dance around its vibrant streets. While exploring Key Biscayne's tranquility and the Everglades' untamed splendor, you'll travel Biscayne Bay's serene waterways.

Miami, though, is more than simply what you see; it's also what you feel. The city's nightlife, food scene, and places for arts and entertainment all reflect its vibrant spirit. We'll direct you to the top locations for dining on culinary delights, dancing the night away, and viewing top-notch theater and musical productions.

In order to make your trip to Miami as easy-going as it is inspiring, we want to give you a thorough guide that combines the pragmatic with the poetic.

We are your go-to resource for information on anything from travel advice to insights into regional cultures.

You can explore these sections to learn more about Miami's core, from its sun-drenched beaches to its secret attractions, from its fine eating to its rich culture. This tour will open your eyes to the magic of Miami, a city that enchants the senses and inspires the soul.

So, as you prepare to set out on an exciting yet tranquil excursion, allow this to serve as your guide through Miami's seductive maze. Now is the time to answer Miami's call. This Miami travel guide for is here to help you learn more about the city's stunning charm.

Welcome to Miami!

It's wonderful to have you here in Miami, the city of dreams.

Miami, Florida, often known as the "Magic City," is a place where fantasy and reality combine, where the ordinary transforms into the extraordinary, and where the sun, sand, and sea meet a wide variety of cultures and experiences. As you start your trip through these pages, I extend a warm welcome to a city unlike any other.

Making Travel Plans

Making the effort to organize your trip can significantly improve how you enjoy the Magic City of Miami once you arrive. Careful planning can help you maximize your journey, whether you're a first-time visitor or a seasoned traveler. The following important actions will guarantee an enjoyable and stress-free trip:

1. Establish Your Travel Dates

Choose a date for your trip to Miami as the first step in the planning process. Despite the city's year-round pleasant weather, it's important to take your tastes into account. Which do you like better:

the sweltering summer, the temperate spring and fall, or the less congested winter? Plan properly because seasonally varying accommodation costs, prominent events, and festivals can affect your trip.

2. Establish a budget

Establish your travel budget. Miami provides a vast selection of lodging, restaurants, and activities to meet different price ranges. Determine how much you are willing to spend on food, hotel, entertainment, and transportation. You may make decisions that are in line with your financial objectives by having a clear idea of your budget.

3. Accommodation

Select the kind of lodging that best meets your needs and price range. From opulent beachfront resorts to quaint inns and inexpensive hostels, Miami has a wide range of accommodations. It's a good idea to make reservations for your lodging in advance, especially during busy tourist times.

4. Transportation

Organize your travel plans to Miami. Miami International Airport (MIA) is the main entry point to the city and offers a wide range of flights. You might also choose to rent a car, use the bus, or rely on ride-sharing services, depending on your plans. Plan your airport trip in advance by researching your options for transportation.

5. Organizing Your Travels

List the activities you want to do during your visit on a rough schedule. A basic strategy can help you make the most of your time, even if it's important to leave room for improvisation. Think about the sights and things to do that interest you, like going to museums, touring South Beach, or trying the local food.

6. Attractions for Research

The must-see sights and secret treasures listed in this guide merit further investigation. Recognize their hours of operation, entry costs, and any upcoming special events or exhibitions. You can plan your daily activities using the information provided.

7. Restaurant Reservations

The richness of Miami's culinary culture is well-known. Make reservations in advance, especially for well-liked dining establishments, if there are any particular places you're keen to sample. Don't forget to sample the regional cuisine, which includes fusion foods, fresh seafood, and Cuban dishes.

8. Travel Insurance

To safeguard your investment from unforeseen circumstances or trip cancellations, think about getting travel insurance. It's a wise precaution to take in order to feel secure while traveling.

9. Packing Necessities

Pack light, breathable clothing because Miami's weather is often warm and muggy. For those hot beach days, remember to pack your swimwear, sunscreen, sunglasses, and hat. Don't forget to pack your passport, ID, and travel insurance information, as well as any other important travel documents.

CHAPTER 1:

Visa and Entry Requirements in Miami

Tourists, business people, and people looking to start a new chapter in their lives frequently visit Miami, Florida. It's crucial to understand the visa and entry requirements that are relevant to your particular scenario in order to ensure a smooth and hassle-free visit or move.

Tourist Visas

Your eligibility for a tourist visa will depend on your nationality if you intend to travel or vacation in Miami. For inhabitants of certain nations, the United States offers the Visa Waiver Program (VWP), which enables them to travel there without obtaining a visa. You may stay for up to 90 days without a visa. Before their trip, travelers from VWP nations must apply for an ESTA, or Electronic System for Travel Authorization.

For citizens of nations not covered by the VWP, a B-2 Tourist Visa will be required. Typically, the application process is filling out the DS-160 form, making an appointment for an interview at the closest U.S. embassy or consulate, and supplying the required papers, such as evidence of your visit's purpose, your financial means, and your ties to your home country.

Business Visas

A B-1 Business Visa is typically necessary if you are traveling to Miami for business. You must finish the DS-160 form, set up an interview, and present supporting documentation, just like for the B-2 visa. These papers must attest to the type of business you are conducting, the length of your stay, and your intention to return home.

Student Visas

You will require a student visa if you intend to attend school in Miami. The F-1 visa for academic studies is the most prevalent type. You'll need to submit a visa application, pay the SEVIS cost, and get an admission letter from a U.S. Institution.

Employment Visas

Employment-based visas, such as the H-1B or L-1 visa, may be appropriate for people who intend to work in Miami. Depending on the type of visa, there may be different criteria and application procedures, so it's vital to seek advice from your potential employer and an immigration lawyer.

Custom Recommendations

Plan in Advance: To allow for processing and potential delays, you must begin the visa application process well in advance of the date you expect to go.

Speak with an immigration lawyer: Consider speaking with an immigration lawyer who can offer specialist advice if you're unsure about the visa application procedure, especially for employment or specialized visas.

Keep Up-to-Date: As regulations might change over time, keep abreast of any updates by monitoring the official websites of the U.S. government.

Travel Insurance: To cover unforeseen medical costs or trip cancellations, it is important to purchase comprehensive travel insurance.

Local Resources: For support and direction once you've arrived in Miami, get in touch with the U.S. Department of State, local immigration offices, or United States Citizenship and Immigration Services (USCIS).

Visa Application

To begin your visa application, adhere to following general guidelines:

Fill Out the Appropriate Online Visa Application Form: Depending on the type of visa, complete the online application form.

Pay the needed Visa Application charge: Depending on the type of visa you're applying for, there may be a needed visa application charge.

Plan an interview: Arrange a meeting with a representative at the American Consulate or in your native country. Attend the interview and be prepared to present biometric data.

Provide Supporting documents: Compile and submit any necessary paperwork, including your passport, photos, and any other documentation pertinent to your trip's objectives.

Attend the Interview: Show up to the interview with the required paperwork and be ready to discuss your trip or anticipated stay in Miami.

Wait for Visa Approval: The consular official will decide whether to approve your visa after your interview. You'll get your visa stamped in your passport if you're accepted.

Please be aware that these stages only give a broad overview of the application process for visas. Depending on the type of visa you're asking for and your place of origin, there may be different requirements and processes. For the most precise and current details on visa application procedures and requirements, always check the official website of the US embassy or the consulate in your country.

CHAPTER 2:

Money and Budgeting for an Affordable Miami Vacation

Miami is a busy and fascinating travel destination that offers a variety of stunning beaches, cultural events, and a buzzing nightlife. However, it's not necessary to go broke to take advantage of everything Miami has to offer. You may enjoy a fantastic vacation without going over budget with smart planning. Here are some suggestions to assist you properly manage your finances and budget for a cheap trip to Miami.

1. Set a Realistic Budget:

Decide how much you can afford to spend on your Miami vacation before you do anything else. Take into account all costs, including lodging, travel, meals, entertainment, and mementos. Making decisions throughout your vacation will be easier if you have a set spending limit in mind.

2. Book Accommodation Wisely:

One of the most expensive components of a trip is occasionally lodging. Consider alternatives like low-cost hotels, hostels, or vacation rentals to save money. Look for lodgings in regions that are a little bit away from the biggest tourist attractions because they frequently cost less.

3. Plan Your Meals:

Particularly in well-known tourist regions, eating out may add up rapidly. To reduce food costs:

Cook a few meals: If your lodging has a kitchen, think about cooking a few of your meals. To cut expenditures on eating out, you can buy goods and create sandwiches or easy recipes.

Investigate Local Eateries: Look for neighborhood eateries and food trucks that provide traditional cuisine at less expensive rates than tourist-oriented eateries.

Look for Deals and Specials: A lot of the restaurants in Miami provide daily or happy hour specials, so look out for them to enjoy meals at a cheaper cost.

4. Use Public Transportation:

Buses and the Metrorail are only two of Miami's effective public transportation options. It's a reasonably priced way to go about town. For further discounts, think about getting a multi-day transit pass, especially if you intend to use public transportation regularly.

5. Explore Free and Low-Cost Activities:

Miami offers a variety of free and affordable activities and attractions. Some ideas include:

Relaxing on the beautiful Miami Beach, which is free to access.

Exploring the *Art Deco Historic District and Ocean Drive.*

Visiting parks like the *Vizcaya Museum and Gardens*, which often have low-cost entrance fees.

Enjoying street art and murals in the Wynwood Walls neighborhood.

6. Plan and Prioritize Activities:

List the experiences and activities that are most significant to you. To take advantage of any discounts, package deals, or other special offers, do your research and make your plans early. This will enable you to prevent impulsive spending on unimportant activities.

7. Buy Less Souvenirs:

Instead of spending money on pricey mementos, think about snapping pictures, compiling a scrapbook, or making a digital memory album. These souvenirs are frequently more price-effective and meaningful.

8. Utilize Travel Apps:

Use travel apps to your advantage to locate offers, discounts, and coupons for a range of events, dining, and transportation.

9. Keep Track of Your Expenses:

During your vacation, keep an eye on your spending. You can keep track of your expenses in real-time with the help of one of the many budgeting applications that are available.

10. Give Flexibility a Chance:

While planning a budget is vital, it's also crucial to keep some money aside for unforeseen costs or impulsive hobbies. Your trip can be more fun if your budget is a little more flexible.

11. Pack wisely:

Making wise packing decisions can enable you to travel on a budget. Make a list of necessities and bring a variety of outfits that go well together. By doing this, you can cut down on the amount of extra clothing or travel-sized products you need to pack for your trip.

12. Exchange of currencies:

If you need to convert money when going abroad, do it at respected currency exchange offices or local banks rather than at the airport, where rates are frequently less advantageous. Due to the competitive conversion rates that credit card providers frequently provide, you can also use your credit card for purchases.

13. Travel Protection:

Even though it may seem like an unnecessary cost, travel insurance can help you avoid financial ruin in the event of unanticipated events like trip cancellation, illness, or missing luggage. Think about getting travel insurance to safeguard your finances and give you peace of mind while you're away.

14. Use credit cards with caution:

Be aware of foreign transaction fees, interest rates, and any other applicable fees while making transactions with credit cards. Look for credit cards that don't charge foreign transaction fees or those that are intended for frequent travelers.

15. Avoid the High Season:

If possible, schedule your trip during the off-peak or shoulder seasons. The price of lodging and activities typically rises when there is less demand.

Additionally, you'll have a more tranquil and uncrowded experience.

16. Sharing Costs with Travel Partners:

Consider splitting the expense of lodging, transportation, and meals if you're traveling with friends or family. This can greatly cut down on your personal costs, making the trip more affordable.

17. Use discounts and coupons:

Before and throughout your vacation, keep an eye out for coupons, discount codes, and special deals. Through numerous travel websites, neighborhood guides, and tourism brochures, you can find discounts for sights, tours, and dining alternatives.

18. Establish a daily spending cap:

Set a daily spending cap to keep your expenses under control. This strategy enables you to stick to your spending plan and prevents overspending while on vacation.

19. Save emergency cash:

Budgeting is important, but you should also keep a little emergency fund on hand in case something unexpected comes up. Unexpected events like a last-minute medical emergency or a change in trip plans can be covered by this fund.

20. Take Group Tours and Packages:

Due to volume bookings and negotiated rates, group tours and holiday packages can occasionally provide financial benefits. Examine these choices to see if they fit your preferences and financial constraints.

In addition to helping you save money, a well-managed budget will also enable you to fully enjoy your trip and develop priceless memories without having to worry about money.

CHAPTER 3:

Must-See Attractions

Miami is home to numerous sites that highlight the city's distinctive fusion of culture, art, history, and unspoiled beauty. Make a list of the must-see sites that will forever change your perception of Miami when organizing your trip to this vivacious city. Here are some of the iconic and culturally significant destinations you won't want to miss:

Miami's South Beach, sometimes known as "SoBe," is the shining gem in the city's crown.

Sun- beaches, a treasure trove of Art Deco buildings, and an electrifying environment that pulses day and night. South Beach is Miami's most colorful and dynamic brushstroke, if Miami is a canvas.

The Art Deco District: An Exhibition

The Art Deco Historic District is one of South Beach's most outstanding features. You'll be transported to a world of pastel-hued structures, neon signage, and elaborate architectural features as you travel along Ocean Drive and Collins Avenue. The optimism and creativity of the time inspired this architectural style, which is distinguished by geometric designs, strong lines, and the use of pastel hues.

The world's largest collection of Art Deco buildings may be seen in South Beach. Many of these structures have undergone painstaking restorations that have kept their antique character. This visual feast is best experienced on foot. To find out more about the significance and history of these structures, you can go on a self-guided walking tour or sign up for one of the guided tours provided by the Miami Design Preservation League.

Ocean Drive is a unique beachside boulevard

The famous boulevard Ocean Drive extends parallel to the shore. It is well known for its sidewalk cafes, outdoor dining, and the vivacious energy in the air. You can eat breakfast, lunch, or dinner here while observing the colorful procession of rollerblades, performing on the street, and classic vehicle aficionados. The neon signs, art deco sidewalks, and famous Colony Hotel are just a few of the elements that make Ocean Drive so distinctively Miami.

Lummus Beach and Park

The Art Deco structures and the sandy Atlantic Ocean coasts are separated from one another by Lummus Park, a gorgeously planted region. It's the ideal location for sunbathing, beach volleyball, and leisurely strolls. With its fine sands and clear waters, the beach is a sunbather's heaven. It's the perfect place to unwind or partake in some enjoyable beach activities because the beautiful ocean begs for swimming and water sports.

The Weekend of Art Deco

If your trip falls in January, you may get to take part in the annual Art Deco Weekend, a festival that honors the neighborhood's distinctive architecture, history, and culture. Live music, vintage vehicles, and guided tours are all available during this event to help you better understand South Beach's rich history.

Entertainment and Nightlife

As the sun sets, South Beach acquires a completely different personality. It becomes a center for entertainment and nightlife. If you're looking for fine cuisine, dance clubs, live music, or peaceful lounges, Ocean Drive and the nearby streets provide it all. The nightlife at South Beach is as exciting and varied as the visitors who visit.

South Beach is more than just a place to visit; it's a captivating combination of history, culture, and unspoiled beauty. It is a location where the past and current coexist harmoniously, where vivid colors, unique architecture, and a buzzing atmosphere produce an intoxicating ambience. South Beach is a wonderful jewel for those looking for an actual taste of Miami's special allure, so it's no surprise that it's frequently the first stop on the road to uncovering the city's charm.

Miami's Little Havana: A Taste of Cuba

In the center of Miami, there is a cultural treasure where the spirit of Havana thrives amid a vibrant tapestry of Latin tastes, vibrant music, and rich customs. Welcome to Little Havana, a part of Miami that offers a fascinating glimpse into the culture of Cuba.

Calles y Café: Exploring Little Havana on foot

Calle Ocho, or Eighth Street, is where Little Havana's essence can be found. There, the distinctive aroma of Cuban coffee permeates the cafes and the strains of salsa music can be heard.

Latin percussion dominates the room. As you stroll down this bustling street, you may come across vibrant murals, craftspeople selling their wares, and even a game of dominoes being played in Maximo Gomez Park with great passion. You can feel the neighborhood's energy, and you'll be surrounded by Cuban sights, sounds, and flavors.

Cuban food is a culinary delight

For those looking for the true flavors of Cuban cuisine, Little Havana is a gourmet heaven. You have a wide range of selections to please your palate, from the well-known Cuban sandwich and hearty ropa vieja to the soothing arroz con pollo. Don't forget to drink a cortadito (Cuban espresso) or a cool mojito with your dinner. For food lovers, the neighborhood is a must-visit because of the mouthwatering variety of flavors offered by its restaurants, cafes, and food booths.

Festival of Calle Ocho: A Cultural Extravaganza

Consider yourself lucky if your trip to Little Havana falls on the Calle Ocho Festival weekend. This yearly festival of Latin culture includes street vendors, live music, dance performances, and art exhibits. It's a wonderful chance to take in the neighborhood's customs and experience it at its most vibrant.

Viernes Culturales: Art and Culture Night

Every month on the last Friday, Little Havana celebrates Viernes Culturales, a cultural event honoring the arts. The galleries and cultural institutions in the area open their doors, giving guests a chance to see Little Havana's artistic side. Live music, dance performances, and a welcoming sense of community fill the streets.

Cultural Centers and Museums

Additionally, Little Havana is home to cultural institutions and museums that provide deeper insights into Cuban heritage. A prominent attraction is the CubaOcho Art & Research Center, which houses a noteworthy collection of works of art, publications, and relics from Cuba. The Cuban Museum offers information on the exile experience and Cuban culture's effect in Miami.

Cigars and Trinkets

Famous throughout the world, Cuban cigars are available for exploration and purchase in Little Havana. Visit cigar establishments and observe the talented torcedores (cigar rollers) creating these renowned cigars by hand. In addition, the area is a great spot to buy souvenirs like classic guayabera shirts and handcrafted crafts.

Music and Dancing

Dance and music are always pulsing in Little Havana. Discover the various locations where you may catch live performances of Latin jazz, son cubano, and salsa. The neighborhood's love of rhythm and movement may be seen in the often unplanned dance parties that take place in the streets.

Little Havana is a thriving, real-world neighborhood that provides an enthralling excursion into the core of Cuban culture. You'll discover that Little Havana is more than simply a location as you relish the tastes of its cuisine, lose yourself in its music, and discover its art and traditions. It is a cultural experience that will leave a lasting impact. It is a small piece of Cuba in Miami, and it invites you to experience its vibrant character.

Art and Culture in Wynwood

Miami is well known for its stunning beaches and energetic areas like Little Havana, but the Wynwood Arts District is a further jewel in the city's cultural crown. Wynwood is a shining example of Miami's vibrant arts community and a place where imagination knows no limitations.

An Outdoor Gallery, Wynwood Walls

The Wynwood Walls, an outdoor gallery that turns everyday walls into stunning canvases, is the focal point of Wynwood's artistic spirit. A stroll through this outdoor artwork resembles a trip through a dreamy landscape. Awe-inspiring artwork by well-known artists from throughout the world is displayed on the walls. The always changing art is a must-see for art fans and anybody who values creativity because it features a variety of genres, from street art to modern.

Studios and Galleries: An Expressionistic Kaleidoscope

Many galleries and artist studios that push the limits of artistic expression may be found in Wynwood. You can discover everything in Wynwood, whether you're drawn to modern paintings, avant-garde sculptures, or experimental mixed-media pieces. It's a place that promotes discovery and engagement with the artistic scene, frequently enabling visitors to interact with artists and have insightful discussions about their work.

Wynwood Art Walk: A Regular Event

Every second Saturday of the month, the Wynwood Art Walk turns the area into a vibrant hub for arts and culture. The streets come alive with performances, live music, food trucks, and art installations as galleries and studios welcome the public inside. You have a one-of-a-kind chance to become fully immersed in the neighborhood's dynamic creative culture.

Murals & Street Art: A Living Canvas

Every turn you make in Wynwood's streets reveals a fresh work of art because they are like a live gallery. Street painters frequent the area, using the walls, doorways, and sidewalks as their canvases. Take your time as you stroll through Wynwood to find the murals, graffiti, and street art that form a dynamic tapestry of color and imagination.

Art Basel in Wynwood: A Global Stage

Every December, Miami Beach is overrun by the yearly international art fair, Art Basel Miami Beach. In addition to hosting satellite fairs, exhibitions, and art projects, Wynwood plays a vital part in this event. The area develops into a major hub for the art world, drawing visitors from all over the world who are interested in art.

Cafes and Restaurants: Fueling the Imaginative Spirit

Wynwood's culinary scene benefits from its creative vitality. The area is home to numerous cafes, restaurants, and food trucks that provide a variety of dining options. Wynwood offers a variety of dining alternatives that are just as diverse as its art scene, whether you're looking for a quick snack, a leisurely meal, or just a coffee break.

Wynwood's Constantly Changing Canvas

Wynwood is a community that never sleeps. Each visit is different due to the ongoing evolution of its art and culture. You may both see and participate in Miami's creative spirit as you explore the murals, galleries, and street art. It is evidence of the city's dedication to artistic expression and a location where you can get a feel for the vibrant beat of Miami's cultural scene.

Wynwood is more than just an arts district; it's a dynamic illustration of the capacity for imagination and innovation in people. Whether you're a seasoned art enthusiast or just looking to immerse yourself in Miami's artistic energy, Wynwood is a riveting location that will leave a lasting impression on your exploration of the city's cultural offerings.

Vizcaya Museum and Gardens

The Vizcaya Museum and Gardens are a tranquil and ageless sanctuary located in the center of Miami, tucked away among the city's lively and busy streets. An enthralling look into the richness and sophistication of a bygone period may be had at this magnificent home.

A Miami Historical Gem

Vizcaya is not merely a museum; it is also a sizable villa built in the early 20th century in the Italian Renaissance style. Industrialist James Deering started construction on this opulent mansion in 1916 and finished it in time for his winter home. It still exists as a reminder of the splendor of the Gilded Age and embodies Deering's idea of a sanctuary with European influences in the middle of Miami.

The Villa: A Palatial Wonderland

You will step into a world of stunning architectural and creative creations as soon as you enter the villa. The Vizcaya interiors are embellished with antique furniture, tapestries, and art collections that capture the spirit of European royalty. The villa's rooms and passageways are examples of the time's craftsmanship and creativity. The sumptuous James Deering bedroom, the luxurious living room, and the peaceful music room are highlights and each offers a window into the past.

The Gardens: A Green Haven

Beyond its villa, Vizcaya is a stunning place with lush gardens and large outdoor areas. The Italian-style gardens include sculptures, fountains, and a wide variety of expertly manicured plants. With spectacular views of the water, the formal gardens give way to a lush tropical forest that leads to Biscayne Bay. The gardens are a work of landscape architecture and welcome guests to explore and take in the peace of nature.

Exhibitions and Special Events

Vizcaya is a vibrant cultural center that hosts a range of events and exhibitions all year long; it is not merely a static museum. It is a vibrant location for fans of art and culture thanks to these activities, which vary from musical performances to art exhibitions. To find out what's happening while you're there, be sure to check the museum's events schedule.

Photography and Filming

Vizcaya is a well-liked tourist attraction because of its gorgeous architecture and scenery. The estate's breathtaking beauty makes it the perfect setting for amateur or professional photographers to capture the beauty of Miami's past.

Today's Vizcaya: A Cultural Gem

In addition to being a historic house, Vizcaya Museum and Gardens is a cultural gem that provides a charming respite from the bustle of modern life. It's a location where you can travel back in time and take in the style and creativity of an earlier time. You will discover that Vizcaya is a timeless haven of old-world elegance and charm in the center of Miami when you explore the villa's rooms and meander around the beautiful grounds.

A trip to Vizcaya is like traveling back in time, when magnificence and beauty were valued highly. Vizcaya Museum and Gardens offers a singular and captivating experience that transports you to a world of elegance and sophistication, whether you're fascinated by history, architecture, art, or simply crave for a tranquil and lovely escape.

Everglades National Park

The Everglades National Park in Miami provides an incredible getaway into the splendor of the natural world. This UNESCO World Heritage Site, which is close to the city, is an example of the distinctive and delicate ecosystem of the Florida Everglades.

A Wetland Wonderland

With about 1.5 million acres of undeveloped wetlands, Everglades National Park is the largest tropical wilderness of any kind in any U.S. national park. There are innumerable types of birds, fish, reptiles, and animals that find sanctuary in this amazing habitat, which is overflowing with wildlife.

Airboat Tours: A Thrilling Adventure

An airboat tour is one of the most well-liked ways to explore the Everglades. You may explore the park's canals, marshes, and mangrove forests in these swift boats as they glide lightly over the water's surface. You might run into alligators, manatees, wading birds, and other local wildlife on your excursion. Insight into the fragile balance of this particular ecosystem is provided by knowledgeable guides.

Wildlife Viewing: A Natural Safari

Wildlife lovers and bird watchers will find heaven in the Everglades. You can explore the park's various habitats thanks to an extensive network of paths and boardwalks. You might see egrets, herons, ibises, and the secretive roseate spoonbill, so keep your binoculars at the ready. If they're lucky, tourists might even get to see the West Indian manatee or the critically endangered Florida panther.

Shark Valley: Cycling Through the Glades

Shark Valley is a fantastic location inside the park for anyone looking for a more active excursion. A 15-mile circle track that travels through the Everglades can be explored here by bicycle. Alligators can be seen lazing in the sun as you pedal along, making for a distinctive combination of outdoor fun and animal observation.

Gator and Wildlife Shows: Educational Entertainment

You may get up close and personal with alligators and other native animals thanks to the numerous wildlife displays and educational presentations provided by airboat tour companies. These interactive activities shed light on the ecology and conservation efforts of the area.

Everglades at Night: Stargazing and Nocturnal Wildlife

When the light goes down, the Everglades' splendor remains intact. It actually acquires a completely new dimension. Due to its designation as an international dark sky park, the area is excellent for observing the stars. It's also a great chance to see nocturnal animals like owls and bats.

Visitor Centers: A Wealth of Information

There are exhibits, movies, and educational displays available in the visitor centers of the Everglades National Park. These resources offer crucial details about the park's history, ecology, and the value of protecting this distinctive habitat.

Conservation Efforts: Protecting a Natural Treasure

The Everglades are essential to keeping southern Florida's ecosystem in balance. A shelter for wildlife and a natural treasure for future generations, this delicate ecosystem is being protected and restored via continuing conservation initiatives.

Planning Your Visit:

Planning your journey appropriately is imperative before visiting the Everglades National Park. Because of the park's size and distinctive features, careful planning is necessary. Verify the park's opening times, entry costs, and any need for special permits or seasonal limitations.

One of the most remarkable ecosystems on earth can be experienced and connected to through the Everglades National Park. It's a location where you may go through untamed countryside while being close to Miami's thriving metropolis. The Everglades have something to offer every traveler and lover of nature, whether they are looking for adventure, wildlife, or calm.

Biscayne National Park

In Biscayne National Park, Miami also enjoys a lovely natural retreat. Only a short drive from the city, this unique national park showcases the beauty and wonder of South Florida's marine life and coastal ecosystems.

A Marine Wonderland

A 173,000-acre tropical wonderland, Biscayne National Park is home to islands, coral reefs, mangrove forests, and pure waterways. The immense width of Biscayne Bay, which offers a haven for marine life and a playground for water sports aficionados, is its main attraction.

Snorkeling and Scuba Diving: Discovering Life Below the Water's Surface

The park is a prime location for snorkeling and scuba diving due to its clean waters and blooming coral reefs. You'll find a rainbow of colors below the surface, from vivid corals to schools of tropical fish. Divers are invited to visit shipwrecks that have been transformed into colorful artificial reefs that are home to a wide variety of marine animals as part of the Maritime Heritage Trail.

Mangrove Trails: A Unique Coastal Ecosystem

Mangrove trees hug the shoreline of Biscayne National Park. Birds, fish, and other creatures can find shelter under these unusual trees. Herons, manatees, and the critically endangered American crocodile can all be seen in the mangroves on guided kayak or boat tours.

Elliott Key and Boca Chita Key: Islands of Adventure

You may go camping, picnicking, and exploring on the park's two main islands, Boca Chita Key and Elliott Key. The elaborate lighthouse on Boca Chita Key, which provides sweeping vistas of the park, is well-known. On Elliott Key, hiking routes wind through the undeveloped countryside, giving outdoor enthusiasts the chance to see the local flora and fauna.

Boating and Kayaking: Waterway Adventures

Kayaking and boating are both excellent activities in the seas close to Biscayne National Park. Bring your own boat or use one that the park rents out. Explore the calm shallows while taking in the calm of the mangroves and the size of the bay.

Bird Watching: A Haven for Avian Enthusiasts

For birdwatchers, the park's various habitats offer a refuge. Numerous bird species, such as pelicans, ospreys, and herons, are seen. There are several options for birdwatching, whether you are trekking the trails, strolling along the shoreline, or discovering the mangrove estuaries.

Protecting a Special Ecosystem via Conservation and Preservation

Southern Florida's delicate marine and coastal ecosystems are greatly protected by Biscayne National Park. The park's biodiversity and natural beauty are being protected via continuing conservation efforts, ensuring that present and future generations can continue to discover and enjoy this special aquatic wonderland.

Practical Advice: Making Visit Arrangements

It's crucial to thoroughly organize your journey before visiting Biscayne National Park. Check the park's opening times, entry prices, and any seasonal or special permission requirements. To further aid in the preservation of this priceless natural gem, familiarize yourself with the best practices for safe water and outdoor leisure.

An aquatic wilderness, Biscayne National Park offers opportunities for exploration and adventure both above and below the surface of its breathtaking seas. You can get in touch with nature there and take in the breathtaking splendor of South Florida's marine and coastal habitats. Whether you enjoy kayaking, camping, snorkeling, or simply being in nature, Biscayne National Park provides an amazing voyage into the wonders of the underwater world.

History and Heritage in Coconut Grove

A Bohemian Oasis

For more than a century, artists, writers, and free spirits have been drawn to Coconut Grove by its relaxed, bohemian environment. One of Miami's oldest communities, the neighborhood's origins may be traced to the late 19th century when it was established by early settlers.

The Barnacle Historic State Park: A Step Back in Time

One of Coconut Grove's historical treasures is The Barnacle Historic State Park. This well-preserved 19th-century house, which originally belonged to explorer Ralph Middleton Munroe, offers a window into Miami's history at a simpler and more primitive time. The park brings history to life by hosting a variety of events and seminars and by providing guided tours.

Historic Streets and Architecture

You'll come across a variety of architectural types as you stroll around Coconut Grove's streets, each of which reveals something about the neighborhood's development. Bahamian and Mediterranean Revival architecture are remnants of the area's illustrious past. Don't pass up the opportunity to explore Charles Avenue, one of Miami's oldest streets, where you'll see quaint old houses.

The Coconut Grove Playhouse: A Cultural Icon

Although it is presently undergoing restoration, the Coconut Grove Playhouse is a significant historical cultural institution that has contributed significantly to the neighborhood's artistic and dramatic culture. The theatre will continue to add to Coconut Grove's rich cultural history after it has been renovated.

The Kampong: A Tropical Oasis

In Coconut Grove, there is a botanical garden called The Kampong that was previously the residence of renowned botanist Dr. David Fairchild. A broad range of tropical plants and trees from different parts of the world may be found in this luxuriant garden. In addition to being a beautiful natural setting, it also reflects the neighborhood's long-standing horticultural ties.

Cultural Events and Festivals

The cultural events and festivals that honor its history and creative spirit are centered around Coconut Grove. For instance, the King Mango Strut Parade offers a hilarious and irreverent perspective on current affairs, while the Coconut Grove Arts Festival brings together artists and art fans from all over the world.

Dining and Entertainment: A Taste of Old and New

The food and entertainment options in Coconut Grove perfectly encapsulate the area's diverse history. It reflects the region's long-standing ties to the arts and culture by fusing classic eateries and pubs with cutting-edge dining options.

Art Galleries and Studios

In its art studios and galleries, Coconut Grove exhibits a creative energy. Explore the neighborhood's many exhibitions and art venues that honor its bohemian and artistic tradition. The area is home to a thriving art scene.

The past and modern mingle in Coconut Grove, creating a lively and diverse community. It is a reflection of Miami's dynamic cultural scene and a testimony to the city's long history. Coconut Grove offers a singular and enriching experience that embodies the spirit of Miami's history and legacy, whether you are drawn to its historic sites, artistic activity, or bohemian environment.

Miami's Historic Architecture

Cuban Influence: Mediterranean Revival

The Mediterranean Revival style is common in areas like Little Havana and Coral Gables. These structures showcase the Spanish and Cuban influences through their red-tiled roofs, stucco walls, and wrought-iron accents. Miami's urban environment is given a dash of Old World charm by the Mediterranean design.

Freedom Tower: A Symbol of Hope

Downtown Miami's Freedom Tower is a significant architectural monument and historical site. The Miami News and Metropolis newspaper's former headquarters were located in this Mediterranean Revival structure. Later on, when Fidel Castro's administration was overthrown, it served as a processing facility for Cuban exiles. Today, it serves as a testament to freedom and hope and is frequently referred to as the "Ellis Island of the South."

The Biltmore Hotel: A Grandeur Reimagined

One of the most recognizable examples of vintage Miami architecture is the Biltmore Hotel in Coral Gables. The hotel's architecture blends elements from Spain and Italy, and its iconic tower soars high into the sky. The Biltmore has a distinguished heritage, having functioned as both a World War II hospital and as a setting for Hollywood movies.

Pérez Art Museum Miami (PAMM): Contemporary Design

Miami has a long tradition of ancient architecture, but it equally values modern design. One such example is the Pérez Art Museum Miami (PAMM). This magnificent museum, created by renowned designers Herzog & de Meuron, has a singular hanging garden and a front that nicely complements the surrounding landscape. PAMM demonstrates the city's dedication to contemporary design and art.

Historic Districts: A Walk Through Time

The MiMo (Miami Modern) District and the Morningside Historic District are only two of the historic neighborhoods in Miami. These locations preserve the design and architecture from each era, providing a window into Miami's shifting identity..

Preservation Efforts: Honoring the Past

Historic structures in Miami are assiduously protected and restored by preservationists and groups. They work to protect the city's architectural legacy so that future generations can enjoy and appreciate it.

CHAPTER 4:

Perfect Beaches

Few natural beauties can compare to the calm, breathtaking beauty of unspoiled beaches. These coastal treasures provide a peaceful getaway into unadulterated nature because they haven't been heavily developed or polluted. For individuals who seek tranquility and inspiration in the natural world, pristine beaches offer a singular and revitalizing experience, from fine white sands to clear waters.

The Glamor of Perfect Beaches

Unspoiled beaches that are frequently tucked away from popular tourist destinations beckon visitors. Their allure is due to:

1. Natural Beauty: Unspoiled beaches are known for their soft, pristine sands, crystal-clear waters, and alluring coastal vistas. These pristine beaches display nature at its most beautiful.

2. Serenity: Far from the commotion of busy tourist hotspots, pristine beaches offer a sense of seclusion and tranquility, making them perfect for rest, meditation, and romantic retreats.

3. Biodiversity: Rich and diverse marine and terrestrial life is frequently supported by the undeveloped ecosystems that surround these beaches. They can be a paradise for snorkeling, birdwatching, or just taking in the beauty of the untainted flora and fauna.

4. Water Activities: Beautiful beaches provide more than simply places to soak up the sun. Activities like kayaking, swimming, scuba diving, and snorkeling are encouraged by the clean seas and abundant marine life.

Sunny Isles Beach

The Miami area's beauty, wealth, and cultural diversity are ideally captured in Sunny Isles Beach, a hidden jewel tucked between Miami and Fort Lauderdale. It is a famous coastal city in its own right and has many traits with its neighbor, Miami Beach.

Magnificent Beaches

Sunny Isles Beach is home to immaculate, broad beaches with fine, fluffy sand and crystal-clear, turquoise waters. These lovely coastlines provide a tranquil escape from the rush of city life, making it the perfect location for anyone seeking leisure and water-based activities. Sunny Isles Beach's beaches are renowned for being pristine, making them ideal for swimming, water sports, and sunbathing.

Luxurious Lodgings

Luxury hotels and expensive beachfront resorts are well known in Sunny Isles Beach. From their lodging, guests can enjoy first-rate service, cutting-edge amenities, and spectacular vistas. The city is a symbol of luxury and draws visitors searching for an opulent and private experience.

Diversity of Culture

Sunny Isles Beach, like Miami Beach, is renowned for its multicultural community. A sizable number of Russian and Jewish populations reside in the area, which adds to its global vibe. Visitors can take advantage of a wide variety of foreign food, cultural activities, and celebrations that showcase the region's diverse cultural heritage.

Luxury shopping

The affluent vibe of the city permeates the retail opportunities. One of the biggest and most opulent retail malls in the area, Aventura Mall is conveniently close by. It offers upscale brands, upscale dining alternatives, and a lavish shopping environment.

Entertainment and the Arts

A cultural hotspot, Sunny Isles Beach is home to various art galleries and events that honor both domestic and foreign artists. Additionally, it is well located for access to the cultural hubs of Miami and Fort Lauderdale, including their museums, theaters, and live events.

Nightlife and Dining by the Water

Sunny Isles Beach's waterfront eating scene is a highlight, providing mouthwatering cuisine and magnificent vistas of the Atlantic Ocean. Bars, lounges, and entertainment venues throughout the city appeal to night owls, making for an equally vibrant nightlife.

Activities and Water Sports

Sunny Isles Beach offers a variety of alternatives for recreational activities and stunning beaches. Visitors can engage in activities including paddleboarding, parasailing, and jet skiing. Yachting trips and deep-sea fishing charters are accessible from the city's marinas.

Parks and Natural Areas

Parks and green places are treasured in Sunny Isles Beach. The city has made investments in exquisitely manicured parks and outdoor spaces that provide a peaceful retreat from the metropolis. These areas offer places to go for family outings, picnics, and leisurely strolls.

With its opulent resorts, immaculate beaches, and ethnic appeal, Sunny Isles Beach is proof of the allure of the Miami area. It is a location that appeals

to tourists looking for luxury, stunning natural scenery, and a variety of cultural experiences. The city is a famous coastal jewel on Florida's southeastern coast thanks to its distinctive blend of grandeur and laid-back beach moods.

Haulover Beach Park

A secret gem off the beaten path along Miami's coast is Haulover Beach Park, located in the thriving metropolis of Sunny Isles Beach. This quiet and untouched location matches the wealth and culture of its surrounding regions and offers both tourists and locals a special natural haven.

Perfect Shorelines

Haulover Beach is well known for its ideal atmosphere and lack of crowds. The Atlantic Ocean's silky, white beaches invite beachgoers to unwind and take in the sun, surf, and cooling ocean breezes. The beach's impeccable condition and breathtaking surroundings are evidence of its dedication to preservation.

Clothing-Optional Section

The clothing-optional area of Haulover Beach Park is one of its distinguishing characteristics. For those who want to experience the beach in its natural state, this location offers a freeing experience as one of Miami's few authorized clothing-optional beaches. It is renowned for its laid-back and inclusive ambiance, which welcomes tourists from all over the world.

Water Sports and Activities

In addition to swimming and tanning, Haulover Beach Park also features surfing and kiteboarding. The Atlantic Ocean's clear waters are ideal for a variety of recreational activities. The park has a marina where guests can book deep-sea fishing trips, rent boats, and engage in other water sports.

Lush Green Spaces

The park's vast green spaces provide a refuge for outdoor activities including picnics and family get-togethers. The groomed grounds are ideal for games, yoga, or just relaxing in the fresh air, while well-kept picnic sites offer respite from the sun.

Family-Friendly Environment

A playground for kids and special spots for family picnics and meetings are available at the family-friendly Haulover Beach Park. All visitors, especially those with children, are in a safe environment thanks to the presence of lifeguards.

Nude Art Show

The park holds an annual Nude Nite Art Show, a distinctive occasion that blends art and a no-clothes policy. Visitors can enjoy artistic expression in a welcoming and open setting thanks to the range of installations, sculptures, and performances it offers.

Haulover Park Marina

A variety of water sports can be accessed from the marina at Haulover Beach Park. The marina offers the tools and accessibility to explore the breathtaking waters of the Intracoastal Waterway and the ocean, regardless of your interest in fishing, boating, or water sports.

Accessibility to Culture and Entertainment

Haulover Beach Park is conveniently situated close to Miami's cultural and nightlife districts while still providing a tranquil nature experience. Visitors may experience Miami and Sunny Isles Beach cuisine, nightlife, and art within a short drive.

The Miami area's wealth and cultural richness are exquisitely complemented by the seclusion of Haulover Beach Park, a natural gem. It offers a serene and welcoming setting where guests may savor the beauty of untainted nature while taking part in a variety of leisure pursuits. Haulover Beach Park offers a special and warm corner of paradise along Miami's coastline, whether you're looking for relaxation, a clothes-optional experience, or a day at the beach with the family.

North Beach

Family-friendly environment

With a number of parks and recreational spaces made to accommodate visitors of all ages, North Beach is a place that is ideal for families. Particularly Allison Park, which has playgrounds, picnic places, and verdant green areas where kids may play and adults can relax, is a well-liked location for family reunions.

Bal Harbour and Surfside

Surfside and Bal Harbour are attractive neighborhoods close to North Beach. These locations are recognized for their high-end dining, shopping, and art offerings. For visitors wishing to experience Miami's better side, Bal Harbour Shops in particular provides upscale shopping, exquisite restaurants, and art galleries.

Coastal Dining

A variety of restaurants are available at North Beach, including waterfront eateries with beautiful ocean views. Visitors can savor international cuisine and fresh seafood while soaking in the tranquil atmosphere of the beach.

Outdoor Activities and Parks

A vast 36-acre park with walking and jogging trails, picnic spots, and breathtaking ocean views is known as the North Shore Open Space Park. The park is popular with both locals and visitors since it provides a chance to get close to nature and participate in outdoor activities.

Entertainment and Nightlife

Compared to South Beach, North Beach tends to be calmer, although it still has entertainment and nightlife alternatives. For a leisurely evening out, visitors can savor live music, cocktails, and seashore bars.

Reachable Peaceful Retreat

A peaceful getaway close to Miami's energetic center is North Beach. It provides a serene and welcoming ambiance that is ideal for people wishing to get away from the throng and unwind in the presence of nature. North Beach offers a tranquil sanctuary in Miami's bustling landscape, whether you're looking for a tranquil beach day, a family-friendly event, or a secluded park to rest.

The Venetian Pool

The Venetian Pool is a charming getaway located in Coral Gables, a charming community just a short drive from North Beach in Miami Beach. This breathtaking aquatic paradise fuses architectural elegance with natural beauty to provide a singular experience that mixes calm and luxury.

Historical Significance

A location rich in history is the Venetian Pool. It was once a coral rock quarry but was changed into a famous swimming pool in the 1920s. A tranquil and picturesque atmosphere is created by the pool's stunning Venetian-style construction, which includes waterfalls, bridges, and lush greenery. It is a symbol of the preservation of architectural history and is included in the National Register of Historic Places.

Unique Features

The Venetian Pool's spring water source is among its most prominent features. A revitalizing and environmentally friendly swimming experience is offered by the daily addition of fresh spring water to the pool. Additionally, visitors can explore the underwater caverns and grottos to add an element of excitement to their stay or observe the two antique lookout towers that provide breathtaking views of the environs.

Relaxing and Friendly to Families

All ages of guests are catered to in the Venetian Pool. It is frequently chosen by families as the perfect vacation spot for a day of rest and entertainment. Children can play safely in the shallow regions of the pool while adults can relax in the deeper areas. The large pool decks offer plenty of space for picnicking and sunbathing.

Features of Waterfalls

The Venetian Pool's flowing waterfalls provide swimming there a distinctive feel. These cascades offer a calming backdrop and foster a peaceful ambiance. The verdant grottos behind the waterfalls can be explored or guests can enjoy them from the pool.

An Exotic Getaway

The Venetian Pool feels like an exotic getaway since it is surrounded by lush, tropical foliage. The palm palms, coral rock formations, and colorful flowers add to the ambience and transport guests to a tranquil and lush paradise.

Activity and Events

Aqua yoga workshops, swimming lessons, and aquatic art sessions are just a few of the events and activities that the pool organizes all year long. It may also be rented privately and is a distinctive location for weddings and other special events.

Coral Gables Discovery

The city of Coral Gables, also referred to as "The City Beautiful," is home to a number of attractions, such as the venerable Biltmore Hotel and exquisite eating establishments. Visitors visiting the Venetian Pool can extend their journey to discover Coral Gables' splendor and culture.In Coral Gables, there is a historic refuge known as The Venetian Pool, which mixes swimming in the open air with stunning architecture. It is a calm and welcoming location where guests may get away from the busy city and lose themselves in a serene and scenic aquatic paradise. The Venetian Pool offers a distinctive and revitalizing escape, whether swimming in the spring water, exploring the waterfalls, or simply relaxing amidst the beautiful surroundings.

CHAPTER 5:

Miami's Laws and Ethics for Visitors

It's important to be aware of the regional regulations and moral standards that support the preservation of this thriving city's distinctive charm while you explore its breathtaking surroundings and different districts. Here is a thorough overview of Miami's laws and morals for tourists:

1. Rules for the Beach:

Some of the most famous beaches in the world may be found in Miami. While taking in the rays, sand, and surf, keep in mind to follow these rules: **Glass Containers Are Not Allowed:** To avoid accidents and injury, glass containers are not permitted on the beach.

Littering: To keep the beaches tidy and beautiful, dispose of waste in the appropriate bins.

Maintain a low level of noise as loud music and other loud noises can bother other beachgoers.

Beach Access: To preserve the delicate coastal habitat, abide by designated pathways and dunes.

2. Drinking Sensibly:

Even though Miami boasts a lively nightlife, it's important to drink responsibly: Alcohol in public places cannot be consumed from open containers in Miami Beach, with the exception of certain occasions.

Driving While Intoxicated: Never do this. Plan a designated driver, use ridesharing or public transit, or all three.

3. Protection of the environment

Since Miami is renowned for its breathtaking natural beauty, it is imperative to preserve and uphold the environment:

Wildlife: Keep a safe distance from the animals and refrain from feeding them because human food can be harmful to their health.

Recycling: Miami encourages recycling; use the appropriate bins for disposal.

Water Conservation: Because of its semi-tropical environment, Miami should save water. Pay attention to how much water you use, especially during dry spells.

4. Road and Traffic Regulations:

Being knowledgeable of local traffic laws is crucial because of the dense traffic in Miami:

Traffic Signals: Follow all posted instructions and signals. Fines may be assessed for disregarding stop signs or red lights.

Pedestrian safety advice includes giving way to pedestrians in crosswalks and using caution in congested areas.

5. Public Conduct:

Miami is a varied and cosmopolitan city, thus it's crucial to show consideration for both locals and guests:

Cultural Sensitivity: Be respectful of the city's many different cultures and receptive to its customs and traditions.

Although Spanish is also commonly spoken in Miami, English is the most common language there. Learning some fundamental Spanish can be respectful and useful.

Tipping: In Miami, tipping is traditional. In cafes and restaurants, a 15-20% gratuity is advised.

6. Maintenance of Historic Sites

It's crucial to respect the historical and architectural importance of Miami's historic neighborhoods and landmarks:

Historic Preservation: Respect historic landmarks and buildings by not damaging them. Laws governing preservation preserve a lot of places.

Appreciate public art, but refrain from touching or climbing on the installations and sculptures.

Marijuana and Alcohol laws:

Specific regulations concerning marijuana and alcohol use are in place in Miami:

Alcohol Sales: Only certain hours, usually after 2 AM, are allowed for the sale of alcohol.

Florida's medical marijuana laws allow for its usage, but recreational use is not permitted. Observe the laws of the state.

Visitors can make sure their vacation to Miami is not only enjoyable but also considerate to the city, its environment, and its citizens by abiding by these laws and moral principles. Responsible tourism makes a pleasant and lasting impression on everyone by preserving the city's appeal and the welfare of its communities.

CHAPTER 6:

Accommodation Options

You must take your lodging alternatives into account when organizing your trip to Miami. You need a comfortable location to stay, but you also need to make sure that it complies with the moral and legal requirements of the city. Miami provides a variety of lodging choices, five-star hotels, accommodations that prioritize the environment. Here is a guide to ethical and convenient lodging in Miami:

1. Hotels and Resorts:

Miami is renowned for its opulent resorts and hotels. You may be confident that your lodging complies with local regulations and moral standards by booking a room at a respected hotel or resort. Many posh hotels are dedicated to sustainability and environmentally friendly techniques, which reduces their influence on the environment.

2. Vacation Rentals:

Miami offers a plethora of vacation rental options, from beachfront condos to stylish apartments. When choosing a vacation rental, opt for platforms that have stringent guidelines and verify the legitimacy of hosts. Ensure that the property you book adheres to the city's safety and zoning regulations.

3. Eco-Friendly Stays:

If you're passionate about sustainable travel, consider eco-friendly accommodations in Miami. Many hotels and lodges are dedicated to responsible tourism, implementing energy-saving measures, recycling, and supporting local conservation efforts.

4. Boutique and Historic Inns:

For a unique and culturally enriching experience, stay in one of Miami's boutique inns or historic hotels. These accommodations often contribute to the preservation of the city's architectural heritage. They maintain the charm of Miami's historic neighborhoods while offering modern amenities.

5. Hostels and Budget Lodging:

Miami offers budget-friendly lodging options, such as hostels and budget hotels. These are perfect for travelers looking to save on accommodation costs, but ensure the establishment is well-maintained and adheres to local laws.

6. Bed and Breakfasts:

Bed and breakfasts provide a cozy and personalized experience, often within the vibrant neighborhoods of Miami. When choosing a B&B, consider the property's reputation and guest reviews to ensure a comfortable and enjoyable stay.

7. Extended-Stay Accommodations:

Extended-stay lodgings, such serviced apartments and corporate housing, provide extra space and services for stays of longer duration. Make careful you pick a dependable supplier who conforms with the law.

8. Safety and Hygiene Standards:

Regardless of your choice of accommodation, always prioritize safety and hygiene. Ensure that the property complies with health and safety regulations and has established cleaning protocols, especially in light of the ongoing COVID-19 pandemic.

Before booking your accommodation in Miami, research your options thoroughly. Read guest reviews, check the property's policies, and confirm that it complies with Miami's laws and ethical standards.

CHAPTER 7:

Hidden Side Attractions

While tourists are familiar with Miami's well-known beaches, vibrant nightlife, and cultural hotspots, the city also features a variety of hidden gems and side attractions that offer uncommon and off-the-beaten-path experiences. You will be able to better appreciate Miami's rich history, diverse culture, and natural beauty by visiting these less well-known areas. Here are a few hidden side attractions in Miami that a responsible traveler should find:

The Secret Gardens of Miami

Beyond Miami's busy streets and vibrant neighborhoods, the area is home to "The Secret Gardens," a collection of obscure natural wonders. These lush refuges offer a tranquil respite from the bustle of the city and a fascinating look at the region's varied flora and animals. A responsible and educational approach to explore Miami's natural beauty is by exploring these hidden gardens. Some of these undiscovered gems are listed below:

1. Fairchild Tropical Botanic Garden:

Tucked away in Coral Gables, the Fairchild Tropical Botanic Garden is a lush and enchanting secret garden, recognized for its commitment to conservation and education. Visitors can explore a diverse collection of tropical plants and rare palms while contributing to the preservation of endangered species.

2. Montgomery Botanical Center:

The Montgomery Botanical Center is a hidden garden devoted to the study and development of tropical palms and cycads, hidden in Coral Gables' gorgeous neighborhood. It is a serene retreat for academics who are passionate about botany.

3. Pinecrest Gardens:

Pinecrest Gardens, formerly known as Parrot Jungle, is a secret haven in the Pinecrest community. This lovely garden has tranquil swan lakes, butterfly houses, and verdant grounds. It provides a fun, informative experience for the whole family while fostering a love of the outdoors and environmental preservation.

4. The Kampong:

David Fairchild's former estate, The Kampong, is tucked away in Coconut Grove. This undiscovered gem provides a peaceful and instructive experience with its outstanding collection of rare and exotic plants.

5. Miami Beach Botanical Garden:

The Miami Beach Botanical Garden, located in the center of South Beach, is a tranquil urban paradise with a variety of plants, art installations, and educational activities that support sustainability and eco-conscious living.

6. Secret Woods Nature Center:

The Secret Woods Nature Center, near Fort Lauderdale, is convenient to Miami and well worth the trip. It encourages environmental education and conservation while providing a tranquil respite into an ecosystem of cypress-maple wetlands.

Not only does going to these hidden gardens allow you to reconnect with nature, but it also encourages ethical travel. Remember to preserve the environment and contribute to the preservation of these tranquil sanctuaries as you discover these hidden natural gems according to the local laws and regulations. These hidden gardens give a better appreciation for Miami's natural beauty and dedication to eco-conscious living by revealing a side of the city that is frequently disregarded.

Jungle Island:

Tropical Flora and Fauna:

The lush ecology of tropical plants, colorful flowers, and unusual trees on Jungle Island transports guests deep into the jungle. Here, you may see the stunning tropical vegetation of Miami, including orchids, bamboo, and native palms, as butterflies and birds flit about the foliage.

Wildlife Encounters:

One of the main draws of Jungle Island is its diverse collection of wildlife. The park is home to a captivating array of animals, including parrots, lemurs, kangaroos, reptiles, and big cats. Visitors can experience up-close and educational encounters with these fascinating creatures while learning about the importance of conservation and animal welfare.

Educational Experiences:

More than just a relaxing getaway, Jungle Island is a hub of knowledge and exploration. The park provides educational talks, wildlife shows, and hands-on exhibits that together help visitors gain a better knowledge of nature and the importance of preserving it for future generations.

Adventure and Exploration:

For those seeking adventure, Jungle Island provides thrilling activities such as ziplining and an obstacle course, all set within a lush and tropical environment. These activities encourage responsible outdoor recreation while respecting the natural surroundings.

Conservation Efforts:

Jungle Island is steadfastly dedicated to ecological preservation and wildlife conservation. By learning about the park's conservation initiatives and making a donation to the preservation of endangered animals, visitors may support these efforts.

Cultural and Historical Significance:

Jungle Island, which was first developed in 1936, has a long history and significant cultural significance in Miami. It has served as a focal point for entertainment, environmental protection, and community engagement. Visitors to the park are able to engage with both the natural environment and the city's history.

Family-Friendly Atmosphere:

Jungle Island is a family-friendly destination, providing engaging experiences for visitors of all ages. Children can enjoy interactive animal encounters, while parents and adults can appreciate the park's dedication to wildlife conservation and eco-conscious practices.

Responsibility in Tourism:

Jungle Island promotes ethical treatment of animals, conservation, and responsible tourism, placing a strong emphasis on these issues. Visitors who go to this attraction and give it support are promoting ethical travel habits that put the health of the environment and its inhabitants first.

Discovering Jungle Island is a trip into the tropical heart of Miami, where luxuriant gardens, a wide variety of wildlife, and eco-friendly activities come together to provide an unforgettable and instructive experience.

Little Haiti

Little Haiti is a hidden cultural gem tucked away in the middle of Miami's urban setting. This thriving neighborhood, which is located just north of downtown Miami, is a monument to the city's impressive ethnic diversity and a shining example of responsible cultural exploration. Visits to Little Haiti offer a special chance to learn about Miami's Caribbean and African roots while showing respect for the neighborhood and patronizing nearby businesses. Here is a sample of Little Haiti's cultural wonders:

Haitian Art and History:

Haitian art and history are concentrated in Little Haiti. Numerous art galleries, studios, and cultural institutions can be found in the area, showing the artistic prowess of Haitian artists. Visitors may take in the vibrant art scene, discover more about the history of Haiti, and recognize how Haitian culture has greatly influenced Miami.

Cultural Events and Festivals:

Throughout the year, Little Haiti is vibrant with a range of cultural celebrations and activities. Visitors can fully immerse themselves in the vibrancy and traditions of Haitian culture by attending these celebrations, which feature musical performances, dance performances, art exhibitions, and gastronomic festivals. Participating in these activities shows that you value cultural diversity and support your neighborhood.

Culinary Delights:

Every culture depends heavily on its food, and Little Haiti offers a unique culinary experience. There are several typical Haitian diners and restaurants in the area where tourists may enjoy regional specialties like griot (fried pig), diri kole (red beans and rice), and hearty, savory soups. Eating in Little Haiti is a chance to celebrate cuisine while also supporting neighborhood businesses.

Local Markets and Boutiques:

Little Haiti features local markets and boutiques that offer a selection of handcrafted goods, clothing, and souvenirs. Exploring these shops allows visitors to appreciate the artisanal craftsmanship of the community and invest in unique, culturally rich keepsakes.

Respectful Cultural Engagement:

Respecting the locals is essential when engaging in cultural research in Little Haiti. It is recommended that visitors approach cultural attractions and events with an open mind and a desire to learn. By observing local traditions, participating in community activities, and patronizing nearby businesses, residents may guarantee that their community flourishes and preserves its rich cultural history.

Artistic Murals:

Little Haiti is renowned for its colorful and expressive murals that adorn the neighborhood's buildings and sidewalks. These works of art offer an instructive and visually interesting experience while celebrating the spirit and tenacity of the Haitian community.

Community Participation:

Little Haiti is a close-knit neighborhood that treasures its heritage. Visitors who are interested in engaging in responsible cultural research can speak with residents, go to neighborhood meetings, and take part in activities that foster harmony and understanding.

Maintaining Cultural Identity:

The preservation of cultural identity in a city that is quickly changing is supported by visiting Little Haiti. Visitors can support Little Haiti's continued success and recognition in Miami's cultural scene by embracing its customs and enjoying Haitian culture.

Visitors can learn about Miami's rich heritage and help preserve a thriving and dynamic community by taking a respectful and educational cultural journey through Little Haiti.

The Ancient Spanish Monastery

Historical Significance:

The 12th-century construction of the Ancient Spanish Monastery in Spain is a live example of the long tradition of European architecture. In the 20th century, it was painstakingly disassembled, shipped over the Atlantic, and painstakingly reassembled in

Miami. You may travel back in time by visiting the monastery and taking in the revenant, inspiring ambiance of a real Spanish medieval monastery.

Cultural Exploration:

Discovering the Ancient Spanish Monastery offers guests a singular cultural experience that not only informs them about the customs and history of Spain but also acts as a reminder of the global influences that have created Miami's cultural landscape. This cultural journey includes the art, architecture, and theological significance of the monastery.

Religious Traditions:

The monastery is still in use as a place of worship and plays an important role in the Miami neighborhood. Visitors are urged to explore the historical and spiritual facets of the location while interacting respectfully with the religious rituals and activities.

Educational Opportunities:

The Ancient Spanish Monastery also functions as a center for education, providing courses and other activities geared toward informing the public about the past, religion, and architecture. These educational programs offer a wealth of information and cultural enrichment.

Respectful Exploration:

Respecting the Ancient Spanish Monastery's historical and religious value requires one to conduct cultural exploration there responsibly. Visitors are expected to abide by the monastery's laws and regulations and respect the religious customs and practices followed there.

Preservation of Architectural Heritage:

It helps to preserve architectural history to visit the Ancient Spanish Monastery. This historical treasure will continue to be accessible to future generations thanks to continuing maintenance and restoration work, which also fosters awe and a respect for the artistry and workmanship of the past.

Supporting Ethical Travel:

Visitors that go to and support the Ancient Spanish Monastery are supporting ethical tourism practices that place a high priority on protecting historic and cultural places. Visitors' donations financially support the monastery's upkeep as well as its educational and cultural programs.

The Ancient Spanish Monastery in Miami provides a chance for responsible tourism and cultural study by acting as a link between the past and present. Its ancient halls, chapels, and courtyards transport tourists to medieval Spain while also promoting the preservation and celebration of architectural and cultural heritage in contemporary society.

Oleta River State Park

Environmental Diversity:

Sand beaches, hardwood hammocks, tidal marshes, mangrove forests, and other natural landscapes are all present in Oleta River State Park. Visitors can encounter a wide range of ecosystems and the abundance of species that resides in them thanks to the environmental diversity.

Outdoor Recreation:

The park provides a wide range of leisure activities that support ethical tourism principles. Hiking, mountain biking, kayaking, paddleboarding, fishing, and swimming are all available to visitors. These pursuits foster a profound respect for the natural world while also protecting it and the creatures that inhabit it.

Educational Experiences:

More than merely a vacation spot, Oleta River State Park serves as a valuable educational resource. The park provides information about the distinctive flora and wildlife of South Florida through educational programs, led tours, and nature walks. Exploring the natural environment responsibly and intelligently is encouraged by these activities.

Cultural and Historical Significance:

Oleta River State Park is notable for its cultural and historical significance in addition to its natural beauty. The Tequesta Indian Mound, a prehistoric archaeological site that sheds light on the area's indigenous past, is located there. Respecting these historical landmarks and understanding their cultural value is a key component of responsible exploration.

Camping and Picnicking:

The park's camping and picnicking areas let guests commune with nature while yet maintaining the ecological balance of the area. These pursuits promote environmentally conscious outdoor enjoyment and emphasize the value of reducing environmental impact.

Water Conservation:

Water conservation is encouraged at Oleta River State Park, which is important given the semi-tropical environment of South Florida. Visitors are urged to use water wisely, particularly during dry spells.

Supporting Reasonable Tourism:

Responsible tourism principles are adhered to when visiting Oleta River State Park. Visitors' fees are used to fund projects aimed at conservation and education, as well as the upkeep and preservation of the park.

Respect for Wildlife:

Many different wildlife species can be found in Oleta River State Park. Exploring responsibly entails keeping a safe distance from animals, not feeding them, and respecting their ecosystems. The varied residents of the park are protected by this strategy.

CHAPTER 8:

Dining and Nightlife

Miami's diverse cultural heritage is reflected in the city's culinary scene. You can enjoy a variety of cuisines, worldwide delicacies, dishes from Latin America and the Caribbean that represent the city's history. Exploring responsibly coincides with participating in a variety of gastronomic adventures.

Miami's Culinary Scene

Diverse Culinary Traditions:

The richness of Miami's food scene is explored. The city's restaurants provide a diverse range of cuisines, from Middle Eastern and Haitian to Cuban and Peruvian. Trying a variety of foods, recognizing their cultural value, and comprehending the stories behind the recipes are all part of responsible dining.

Farm-to-Table Dining:

The farm-to-table movement, which emphasizes the use of locally sourced, fresh ingredients, is embraced by many Miami eateries. You may help local farmers and lessen the environmental impact of long-distance food transportation by eating at these places.

Sustainable Seafood Choices:

The seafood scene in Miami is a highlight because of its proximity to the water. Responsible seafood consumption entails choosing species that are harvested in a manner that is environmentally beneficial. This promotes both the wellbeing of the oceans and local fishermen's means of subsistence.

Local Businesses and Artisanal Products:

Choosing locally owned eateries, cafes, and markets will help you explore Miami's culinary scene. These establishments frequently give back to the neighborhood and highlight handcrafted goods, which speaks to the distinctive culture of the city.

Cultural Awareness:

Respecting the ethnic subtleties of food is another aspect of responsible dining in Miami. It's crucial to approach different cuisines with an open mind and a willingness to learn about the etiquette and cultural customs that go along with each dish.

Consuming Food Ethically:

Consider practicing ethical food consumption as a responsible traveler by reducing waste. When ordering, choose a smaller portion and use takeout containers if necessary. Food waste is decreased as a result.

Sustainable Dining Practices:

Many Miami restaurants are implementing environmentally friendly measures like lowering plastic waste, conserving electricity, and water management. Supporting these businesses helps make the city more environmentally friendly.

Supporting Ethical Initiatives:

Many Miami restaurants are implementing environmentally friendly measures like lowering plastic waste, conserving electricity, and water management. Supporting these businesses helps make the city more environmentally friendly.

Assisting with Moral initiatives:

Some restaurants in Miami combine their business practices with moral and charitable concerns. In addition to providing a distinctive dining experience, going to these places helps businesses that are actively promoting social change.

Alcohol Use in Moderation:

Responsible drinking is essential while taking advantage of Miami's nightlife. To ensure safety and wellbeing while engaging in your culinary discoveries, appropriate and moderate alcohol intake is essential.

Culinary Education:

Seeking out culinary experiences that inform guests about the background and traditions of the dish is another way to engage in responsible dining. Many restaurants provide workshops or other interactive experiences that let you get involved in the cooking process.

The city's multicultural heart is deliciously explored through Miami's food scene. Responsible visitors may help preserve and celebrate Miami's unique culinary heritage by relishing its variety and mouthwatering options while supporting neighborhood businesses, honoring cultural norms, and making eco-friendly decisions.

Ocean Drive Dining

Ocean Drive is more than just a charming section of South Beach in Miami; it's also a gastronomic destination that combines the city's cuisine with stunning coastal vistas. Responsible dining on Ocean Drive entails enjoying Miami's gastronomic treats while simultaneously preserving the area's natural beauty and helping the neighborhood. Here are some tips for dining responsibly on Ocean Drive:

Oceanfront Eateries:

Oceanfront dining is available at many of Ocean Drive's eateries. Enjoy the breathtaking views of the Atlantic Ocean while dining. It's important to enjoy nature's beauty while dining responsibly.

Diverse Culinary Offerings:

A variety of culinary cultures, including Latin American, seafood, and foreign cuisine, are represented in the Ocean Drive dining scene. A responsible exploration promotes eating new foods while honoring their cultural value.

Sustainable Seafood:

Due to Miami's coastal location, seafood is in plentiful supply. Making ethical seafood choices, promoting ethical fishing methods, and preserving the oceans are all part of responsible dining.

OutdoorDining:

The outdoor dining spaces and sidewalk cafes along Ocean Drive add to the area's appeal. Utilizing these outdoor areas allows responsible visitors to eat their lunch while lowering the demand for climate control.

Sizzling Nightlife: Clubs and Bars

Miami has a renowned nightlife, and the heart of the city's nocturnal vitality can be found in its clubs and bars. In addition to ensuring a pleasant time, responsible revelry in Miami's bustling nightlife scene also protects everyone's safety and the preservation of the energetic environment. How to responsibly enjoy Miami's nightlife is as follows:

Diverse Nightlife Scene:

High-energy dance clubs, quaint cocktail bars, and everything in between can be found in Miami's nightlife. In order to enjoy various environments and support various enterprises, responsible travelers might explore the varied possibilities.

Local Talent:

Local DJs, musicians, and performers are frequently featured at Miami clubs and pubs. Taking in their performances encourages local artists and highlights the brilliance of the area.

Responsible Alcohol Consumption:

Responsible and moderate drinking should be practiced. Know your limitations and use designated drivers or ride-sharing services if needed. This guarantees that everyone will be safe.

Lively Latin Music and Dance

Dining in Miami is a multi-sensory experience that includes tastes, sights, and noises in addition to the actual cuisine. Your culinary adventure takes on an exciting new dimension thanks to the city's vibrant Latin music and dance scene. Your dining experience can be improved as you support the local arts scene by participating responsibly in this dynamic cultural aspect. Embrace the vibrant Latin music and dancing in Miami's dining scene by following these steps:

Live Latin Music:

Live Latin music performances are frequently heard in Miami restaurants, giving a lively and rhythmic flavor to your meal. Tourists who behave responsibly can take in these concerts while supporting regional artists and venues.

Dance Rhythms:

Salsa, merengue, and bachata are just a few of the dance rhythms that are frequently associated with Miami's Latin music industry. Respecting the traditional significance of these dances, please participate in the enjoyment if you feel the urge to dance.

Respecting Performers:

Respecting the performers is a necessary component of enjoying Latin music and dance responsibly. To support their livelihoods, congratulate them on their skills, buy their songs, or buy their products.

Cultural Awareness:

Consider studying about the beginnings, significance, and history of different dance styles to fully understand the rich cultural diversity of Latin music and dance. Miami frequently hosts dancing events and workshops where you can learn more.

Responsible Dancing:

If you participate in the dance, keep in mind to conduct yourself responsibly. Respect your fellow dancers and follow the guidelines set forth by the venue.

CHAPTER 9:

Shopping and Entertainment

Miami's Malls

Miami is not only a center for food and nightlife, but it is also a shopping haven with malls that feature a mix of upscale premium brands and one-of-a-kind boutiques. Shopping responsibly at Miami's malls means having fun while promoting regional companies and being aware of your environmental impact. What you should know about Miami shopping:

Diverse Shopping Destinations:

There are many places to shop in Miami, from expensive malls like Bal Harbour Shops to hip boutiques in Wynwood. Responsible shoppers can look in many places to find a choice of fashion and design.

Supporting Local Businesses:

There are numerous local stores and designers in Miami's retail landscape. By making purchases at these businesses, you help the neighborhood economy and encourage the fashion and art scene in Miami to be creative.

Quality Over Quantity:

Overindulge in quality over quantity. In order to lessen the environmental impact of rapid fashion, responsible buying entails investing in items that you'll value and use for a long time.

Community Engagement:

Participate in neighborhood gatherings, pop-up stores, and fashion shows that highlight local designers and artists and advance the Miami fashion and arts scene.

Responsible Consumption:

By using reusable bags, avoiding single-use plastic, and making wise purchase decisions, conscientious consumers may reduce waste.

Appreciating Local Culture:

The unique culture and heritage of Miami are frequently reflected in the city's commercial environment. Respecting the customs and significance of diverse designs and styles will help you approach your shopping experience with cultural sensitivity.

Sustainable Practices:

Shop at establishments that employ environmentally friendly procedures like recycling and energy conservation. Others are inspired to support you by doing the same.

Unique Boutiques in the Design District

The Design District in Miami is a haven for fashion enthusiasts and art aficionados alike. It's a place where shopping becomes a work of art, and responsible consumerism takes center stage. Exploring the district's unique boutiques provides an opportunity to support local designers, appreciate artistic craftsmanship, and engage in retail therapy with a responsible twist.

Artful Retail Experience:

The Design District offers an artful retail experience, where fashion, design, and artistic expression converge. Responsible shoppers can engage in a cultural and creative journey while respecting the unique character of each boutique.

Supporting Local Designers:

Many boutiques in the Design District feature local designers and artists. By shopping at these establishments, you support the creative talent of Miami's fashion and art community.

Entertainment: Theater and Concerts

As diverse and exciting as the city itself, Miami offers a wide variety of entertainment alternatives. From top-notch theaters to live performances, Miami's responsible appreciation of the performing arts enriches the city's cultural landscape and supports regional performers. Following are some guidelines for attending theater and concerts responsibly:

Theater Productions:

From traditional plays to cutting-edge modern acts, Miami's theaters present a diverse spectrum of productions. While appreciating the craft and creativity of the performances, responsible theatergoers may help out their community's actors, directors, and theater groups.

Cultural Appreciation:

Miami's theaters frequently present shows that highlight the city's diverse cultural heritage. Respect the provided customs and narratives, and approach each show with cultural awareness.

Live Concerts:

With a variety of concerts and performances taking place all year long, Miami is a live music mecca. Supporting both domestic and foreign musicians, as well as the performance venue, are important components of attending concerts responsibly.

CHAPTER 10:

Informative Content

Weather and When to Visit

One of Miami's most enticing characteristics is its temperature, which makes it a desirable location all year long for a variety of entertainment options like theater, concerts, shopping, and more. To guarantee you have the best experience, it is crucial to understand the weather and know the best times to visit Miami.

Miami's Year-Round Appeal:

Miami experiences tropical rainfall, which means it is generally warm and has a distinct wet season. It is a year-round destination for a range of entertainment activities due to its climate.

Winter (December to February):

Miami's busy season is in the winter. The mild and sunny weather is ideal for outdoor amusement and activities. There are lots of concerts and cultural events going on, and the theatrical scene is very active. Just keep in mind that this is the busiest time of year in Miami, so planning ahead for your theater tickets and lodging is recommended.

Spring (March to May):

Miami's spring season is a wonderful time to do outdoor shopping, attend concerts, and take in the vibrant local culture. The crowds begin to thin out compared to the winter months, and the weather is warm and pleasant.

Summer (June to August):

Although Miami's summer season falls during its rainy season, this does not mean that the city's entertainment industry slows down. Summer is a fantastic season to see indoor concerts and theater productions. An occasional thunderstorm as well as afternoon showers are to be expected.

Fall (September to November):

It's a wonderful time for outdoor shopping and concerts in Miami during the fall because it's a transitional season with less rain. If you intend to go at this period, you must be aware of the weather since the hurricane season peaks around September.

Choosing the Right Time:

Your interests will determine when is the ideal time to visit Miami for theater, music, and shopping. Winter is the best time to travel if you like pleasant weather and don't mind large people. The weather and crowd levels are best in the spring and fall. Although the summer can be humid, it's a great time to enjoy indoor entertainment.

Weather Considerations:

Due to the humid environment of Miami, you should be ready for high temperatures and sporadic rainfall, especially during the wet season. It's best to wear loose-fitting clothing and to have rain protection on hand.

Accommodation and Ticket Reservations:

Regardless of when you intend to travel to Miami for entertainment, it is imperative to reserve lodging and event tickets in advance. By doing this, you can be sure that you'll get the greatest selections and a smooth experience.

Miami's weather makes it easy to have fun all year long, and the best time to visit will largely depend on your preferences. Miami's climate and seasonal changes are significant variables to consider to make the most of your trip, whether you're going to a concert, seeing a play, shopping in boutiques, or taking part in other forms of entertainment.

Safety Tips

1. Be Aware of Your Surroundings:

Always be on the lookout whether you're out shopping, at a concert, or seeing a play. Be aware of your surroundings and follow your instincts.

2. Plan Ahead:

A safe and pleasurable event requires careful planning. Understand the event schedule, transportation alternatives, and venue locations. Share your intentions with a friend or a family member.

3. Use Authorized Ticket Sellers:

Buy event tickets only from authorized dealers and official sources. Avoid scalpers and illegal resellers.

4. Stay in Well-Lit Areas:

While exploring Miami's entertainment and cultural offerings, stick to well-lit and populated areas, especially at night.

5. Keep Priceless Items Safe:

Keep your stuff safe when shopping or attending events. Be careful with your personal items and carry crossbody bags or money belts.

6. Drinking sensibly:

Do it responsibly if you decide to drink alcohol while attending entertainment events. Know your boundaries and, if required, make arrangements for a designated driver or ride-sharing service.

7. Respect Local Laws:

Learn about local laws and ordinances, such as those concerning traffic and open containers. Following these rules will guarantee your safety.

8. Emergency Contacts:

In case of any unplanned occurrences, save emergency contact information, such as the local police and medical services, in your phone or keep it nearby.

9. Stay Hydrated:

Staying hydrated is essential, especially when participating in outdoor activities and events in Miami's sometimes hot and muggy climate.

10. Weather Awareness:

Keep an eye on weather conditions, especially during hurricane season. Be prepared for sudden weather changes, and follow safety guidelines if necessary.

11. Use Reputable Transportation:

When going around the city, use trustworthy transportation choices like authorized taxis or ride-sharing services. When taking rides from strangers, use caution.

Useful Phrases

Navigating Miami's entertainment and cultural scene becomes more enjoyable and secure when you have a few useful phrases at your disposal. While English is widely spoken in Miami, the city's multicultural environment can make knowing a few phrases in other languages helpful. Here are a few phrases to consider:

English:

1. "Can you suggest an excellent restaurant nearby?"

2. "Where's the nearest bus/metro station?"

3. "I need a taxi to [destination]."

4. "Is there a medical facility nearby?"

5. "Can you help me find my way to [venue]?"

Spanish:

1. "¿Puede sugerirme un buen restaurante cercano?" (Can you suggest an excellent restaurant nearby?)

2. "¿Dónde está la estación de autobús/metro más cercana?" (Where's the nearest bus/metro station?)

3. "Necesito un taxi a [destino]." (I need a taxi to [destination].)

4. "¿Hay una instalación médica cercana?" (Is there a medical facility nearby?)

5. "¿Puede ayudarme a llegar a [lugar].?" (Can you help me find my way to [venue]?)

Creole (Haitian Creole):

1. "Eske ou ka rekòmande yon bon restoran tou prese la?" (Can you suggest an excellent restaurant nearby?)

2. "Kote estasyon autobis/metro ki pi pre?" (Where's the nearest bus/metro station?)

3. "Mwen bezwen yon taksi pou ale nan [destinasyon]." (I need a taxi to [destination].)

4. "Eske gen yon sant medikal nan katye a?" (Is there a medical facility nearby?)

5. "Eske ou ka ede m 'jwenn wout la nan [lokasyon]?" (Can you help me find my way to [venue]?)

The following terms and phrases might make it easier for you to communicate and move around, whether you're looking for directions, advice, or need aid. Although Miami is renowned for its vibrant cultural scene, using these words will enhance your visit and ensure that you are respectful of the local way of life.

Emergency Contacts

Emergency Contacts for a Safe Stay in Miami

Being able to reach the appropriate emergency contacts might significantly impact your ability to stay safe while taking in Miami's entertainment and cultural scene. Save these crucial emergency numbers to your phone so you always have them with you when you're in the city:

1. Emergency Services: 911

For quick assistance from the police, fire, or medical services in any emergency, contact 911. The emergency hotline for any situation is at this number.

2. Non-Emergency Police:

For non-emergency situations or to report incidents that don't require immediate attention, contact the local police department in Miami. Be sure to have their non-emergency contact number saved.

3. Medical Emergencies: Local Hospitals

Be aware of the nearest medical facilities or hospitals, and have their contact information on hand in case of medical emergencies.

4. U.S. Coast Guard:

If you're near the coast and encounter a maritime emergency, the U.S. Coast Guard can provide assistance and rescue services. Know their contact number.

5. Consulate or Embassy:

If you're an international visitor, be aware of the contact information for your country's consulate or embassy in Miami. They can provide assistance in case of legal or travel-related emergencies.

6. Transportation Services:

In case you need assistance with transportation, keep the contact numbers for local taxi services, rideshare apps, or public transportation services available.

7. Travel Insurance Contact:

If you have travel insurance, keep your policy information and the contact number for your insurance provider on hand for any travel-related emergencies.

8. Lost or Stolen Items:

In case you lose personal belongings or experience theft, be sure to have the contact information for local authorities or reporting services.

9. Roadside Assistance:

If you're using a rental car, having the contact number for roadside assistance can be essential in case of car trouble.

10. Local Tourist Information Centers:

In Miami, there are numerous tourist information centers that can offer advice and direction if you run into problems or need local knowledge.

It's essential to be aware of and have access to these emergency numbers for a secure and happy trip to Miami. Even though it's rare that you'll require them, being ready can provide you peace of mind and guarantee that you have the tools you need in case of any unforeseen circumstances.

Packing Essentials

1. Lightweight Clothing:

Miami experiences warm weather all year round. Pack lightweight, breathable clothing, such as shorts, tank tops, sundresses, and swimwear. Don't forget comfortable walking shoes for exploring.

2. Sun Protection:

Miami's sun can be intense. Bring sunglasses, a wide-brimmed hat, sunscreen, and lip balm with SPF to protect yourself from the sun's rays.

3. Rain Gear:

Miami experiences occasional rain showers, especially during the wet season. To remain dry, bring a small umbrella or a lightweight rain jacket.

4. Evening Attire:

If you plan to attend theater performances, concerts, or fine dining, consider packing some dressier attire. Miami's nightlife can be glamorous, so it's a good idea to have some evening options.

5. Swimsuit and Beach Gear:

Miami's beaches are a must-visit. Don't forget your swimsuit, flip-flops, and beach essentials like a beach towel, sun hat, and beach bag.

6. Travel Adapters:

If you're visiting from a different country, ensure you have the appropriate travel adapters to charge your devices and power your electronics.

7. Travel Documents:

Keep your travel documents, including your passport, ID, flight tickets, and hotel reservations, in a secure travel wallet.

8. Medications and First Aid Kit:

If you have prescription medications, pack an ample supply for your trip. Additionally, bring a basic first aid kit with essentials like band-aids and pain relievers.

9. Local Currency: -

While many places in Miami accept credit cards, having some local currency on hand can be useful, especially for small purchases and tips.

10. Language and Phrase Guides:

Consider bringing language and phrase guides, especially if you plan to interact with people in languages other than English.

11. Entertainment Options:

Don't forget your entertainment options for downtime, such as books, e-readers, or portable devices for streaming or music.

12. Responsible Travel Attitude:

While not a physical item, adopting a responsible and respectful travel attitude is essential for making the most of your Miami experience.

BONUS

An Itinerary covering Miami, Florida in six days.

Day 1: Exploring South Beach

Morning: Take a stroll along Ocean Drive and the well-known South Beach to start. Enjoy the sunshine, the stunning art-deco buildings, and the recognizable lifeguard towers.

Lunch: Enjoy a Cuban sandwich at a nearby café.

Afternoon: Go to the Art Deco Historic District. For more on the architecture, stop by the Art Deco Welcome Center.

Evening: Discover the vibrant nightlife along Ocean Drive. For a fun meal, try one of the hip eateries.

Day 2: Miami Beach and Waterfront

Morning: Spend the morning at Miami Beach, which is immaculate. Sunbathe, go swimming, or engage in some water activities.

Lunch: Visit a coastal restaurant and get some fresh fish.

Afternoon: Explore the Bass Museum and the Art Basel at Collins Park to take in some culture and the arts.

Evening: Take in the sunset while strolling the Miami Beach Boardwalk.

Day 3: Little Havana and Culture

Morning: Explore Little Havana. Enjoy a café cubano while visiting the renowned Domino Park.

Lunch: Dine on authentic Cuban food at a nearby restaurant.

Afternoon: Discover Cuban culture firsthand in the Little Havana Art District.

Evening: Visit Ball & Chain or Hoy Como Ayer to see a live dance or music performance.

Day 4: Cultural Exploration

Morning: Enjoy contemporary and international art by going to the Pérez Art Museum Miami (PAMM).

Lunch: Visit Verde, PAMM's restaurant, and sample some Latin-inspired cuisine.

Afternoon: Learn about Wynwood Walls' thriving artists community, which is well-known for its street art and galleries.

Evening: Get dinner at a trendy restaurant in Wynwood.

Day 5: Natural Beauty and Shopping

Morning: Go to Key Biscayne. Visit Bill Baggs Cape Florida State Park and ascend to the top of the ancient lighthouse.

Lunch: Visit a restaurant along the coast for lunch.

Afternoon: Try kayaking or paddleboarding, or go to the neighboring Crandon Park Beach.

Evening: Once on the mainland, indulge in some retail therapy at Bayside Marketplace.

Day 6: Adventure and Departure

Morning: Take advantage of the opportunity to see wildlife, an airboat ride, and an Everglades tour.

Lunch: Explore the Everglades region's native food.

Afternoon: Explore the old Venetian Pool in Coral Gables by taking a leisurely trip there.

Evening: Retire to your accommodation once more, unwind, and get ready to go.

CONCLUSION

Your Unforgettable Miami Experience

As your stay in Miami draws to a close, take some time to consider the intricate embroidery of memories you have created. You may be sure that Miami, a city that combines cultural diversity, breathtaking natural beauty, and exciting entertainment, has made an everlasting impression on your heart.

Throughout your visit, you've walked Ocean Drive's bustling bustle, feeling the pulse of Miami's nightlife echo in the streets of South Beach. You've enjoyed Miami Beach's golden sands, letting the sun's warmth caress your skin and the sound of the waves calm your spirit.

You have experienced the warmth and vitality of Cuban culture by dancing to the beats of Cuban music, sipping cafecito, and indulging in real cuisine in Little Havana. Additionally, you have experienced Miami's cultural and ecological wonders as you strolled through Wynwood's contemporary art district and the calm serenity of the Everglades.

You were able to observe this vibrant city's architectural wonders, like the Art Deco Historic District and the famed Venetian Pool in Coral Gables, while you traveled about it. Of course, you couldn't resist the temptation of indulging in delectable regional fare, such Cuban sandwiches, fresh seafood, and meals with a Latin influence.

Your eyes have been awakened to the beauty of other cultures thanks to Miami's multicultural identity, and its numerous neighborhoods have exposed you to a wide range of viewpoints, tastes, and colors. You have felt Miami's distinct charm, whether you got lost in the complex beauty of Little Havana or the captivating murals of Wynwood.

As you say goodbye to Miami, keep in mind the welcoming people you met, the many different languages you heard, and the amazing sights, sounds, and flavors that have made it your home away from home.

Your wonderful trip to Miami will leave you with a wealth of lifelong memories rather than just a collection of fleeting moments. It serves as both a reminder of the endless opportunities that come with discovering a city as diverse as Miami and a call to return in the future and uncover even more of its enchantment. Till then, goodbye, and may the experiences you had in Miami fuel your wanderlust and hunger for learning about different cultures.

Rafael M. Stones.

Made in United States
Orlando, FL
03 December 2023

40020552R00072